IN THE

IN THE
CRUEL ARCADE

Alan Brownjohn

SINCLAIR-STEVENSON

First published in Great Britain in 1994
by Sinclair-Stevenson
an imprint of Reed Consumer Books Ltd
Michelin House, 81 Fulham Road, London SW3 6RB
and Auckland, Melbourne, Singapore and Toronto

A CIP catalogue record for this book is available at the British Library

ISBN 1 85619 3977

Typeset by Deltatype Ltd, Ellesmere Port, Cheshire
Printed and bound in Great Britain
by Cox and Wyman Ltd, Reading, Berks

i.m.
G.M. MacB.

Contents

I

II

ACKNOWLEDGEMENTS

are gratefully made to the following, in which these
poems, or versions of them, previously appeared:
Acumen, Agenda, Ambit, Elected Friends (Poems
for and about Edward Thomas, ed. Anne Harvey),
Equivalencia, A Garland for Stephen Spender (ed.
Barry Humphries), the *Independent, London
Magazine, London Review of Books,* the *Magpie
Press, New Statesman and Society,* the *Observer,
Outposts,* the Poetry Book Society anthologies,
1989 and 1992, the *Haiku Quarterly,* the *Spectator,
Thames Poetry,* the *Times Literary Supplement,
Turret Bookshop.*

I

A Pride

In a cold October twilight, down towards
An estuary beach of mud and stones,
Three lifelong friends lurch and scramble over banks
Of red soil fallen from cliffs which one afternoon,
Fifty years ago, broke and carried the whole of a church,
Its churchyard, and half a road to the shores below.

They plunge headlong on crumbling cakes of earth
Where tipped-out garbage has mingled with the rubble,
And grass and painful gorse grown over it;
And sometimes they can't keep upright, and have to slide
On their arses with their hands thrown out to grab
At the fragile vegetation. But finally

They arrive at the river, and slither on the stones
— Which turn out to be nothing more than heavy
Medallions of mud shaped by the lapping tides . . .
The scum of the water nudges at their shoes,
And why did they come here, dangerously treading
The remains of fifty years? It is getting dark,

And they have to lug their bodies up again,
Up all that distance to the eroding edge
Of the cliff again, in unspoken competition,
With care to avoid the crevasses under the grass.
There is, and there has been, no kind of point or pleasure
For legs or lungs or spirits in any of this,

Though when they can breathe at the top, looking down across
The tracks by which they ascended, there is a pride
In their sweating faces. And yet, by themselves,
With no one else at the end of the day to admire them,
Or even convert them to symbols, why did they want
To do it, they ask? — After all, it was getting dark.

The Last Stone

Moving from hope to hope like stepping-stones,
One day the eyes and feet discovered
That the next step was too huge, they'd reached the last
Stone possible to reach and would stand there always,
Exhausted by that very last lunge forward
Onto its narrow, dry security;
And there would be nothing left to do, but stand
With your shoes having, so far, kept out all the water;
But with your expensive threadbare trousers threaded
By a rising wind, and your little jacket round you
Not enough to keep the cold out; and try, and try,
To hope, to *hope*, you could retain your balance;
This being only half-way across the river . . .

Barto

Beyond the door the green arrow pointed at,
Was one of the dankest human corridors:
Cold, short; one lightbulb swinging unshaded
In a draught from an unseen direction;
No telling what was paint and what was stain;
No guessing what might be roped up inside
The scruffy baskets pushed into that alcove,
Or what the liquid spilt from them might be;
A half-world not to stand mesmerised in,
But no going back to the door of entry
And the first warm place.

                  There is another door,
Leading out to sounds which might be traffic
Or might be the sea at the foot of a cliff,
And that is where the draught is coming from,
An invitation to an ultimate cold . . .
I comb my hair, make sure my back is straight,
And press the tired flesh of my face to smile
As I do not Push Bar to Open.

Graveside

Our faces show we disapprove profoundly.
He should never have brought us all to this
On a summer's day. Or any other day.
It is as if he were setting out to shock.
He could have found other ways of reminding us.

– Though for all his nerve, we remain superior,
Outnumbering him, and still in a position
To discuss this rare disaster.
                              If we all put
Our heads together, surely we could devise
Some precautions to take against it, soon!

Until You Look

All those perfect white dots are perfectly still,
Like bits applied by a brush until I look
And see them flap and fidget separately,
Rise up, veer round, resettle. The marsh down there
Is also painted, until I look and find
That all its turrets of green, the gorse, the samphire
And all the fawn tufts of grass, shake negative heads.
I swear the clouds haven't moved all afternoon,
But unless the background sky has shifted . . .
I look, and under any kind of calm,
Each hand that restrains on an arm or calms on a forehead,
Is a perpetual restlessness, a hurrying
Towards the end; which only consciousness
Can be terrified of and want to put a stop to.

On the Death of Margaret Lockwood

All the old picture girls are dying,
The proud posed queens
Of the magazines under the cushions,
The black-and-white touched up
Ladies of all the Annuals.
Soft millions of dots
In a thousand photographs
Have smiled past one final gazer.

I like to think he too
Begged heads to turn
And face him and lips to smile,
And found his avid eyes
Distracted by useless words
In the printed captions:
And for a second, thought
Of having second thoughts.

A Corridor

Several layers of paint never did
Turn the wall in the scullery the matching
Deep green Dad wanted, in the end
It was always pale and peculiar again.
One night there was a hole leading through to a space
Going on and on like the one in the hospital,
With the endless shelves I was told I came from.
On better nights it became the carpeted
Avenue in the basement of the store
Past the springy double beds and the sofas,
And ended where it narrowed between mirrors
Hung both sides head-high down a dimmer stretch
Where people turned their heads all the way along.
I followed it, it changed to an arcade
With tatty lawn-strips of an artificial
Deep green grass. At a counter we stood around,
With a kind of cruel and watchful aunt in charge,
The ping pong balls sprayed up in different colours
From out of a fountain, looking something like
The constituent planets in a diagram
Of the unsplit atom. They dropped if you were lucky
To end up in the small nets you presented
On the ends of bamboo sticks, nets made
Of a tearable fabric like an Xmas
Stocking in a shop, or a big girl's stocking:
You won a money prize for six balls safely
Caught in your net. I would stand for half-an-hour
Or as long as my pennies lasted, but I lost
My money in the end. I always finished
With my net nearly empty, and the woman sent me
Away from her counter to a deep green wall,
Or not a wall, a hole or door which opened
Onto a corridor like the hospital's,
The endless one with all the endless shelves
Where I, they told me whenever I asked,
Had been a dot slowly growing a long long time.

Waterloo

On Monday the automatic *Mind the Gap*,
Which sounds out with a sudden hectoring roar,
Didn't speak. 'Don't they care,' said some grey-haired chap
I thought I'd seen on stage at the Cottesloe,
'If we all go plunging down?' His two old feet
Were dithering humorously, but even so
He minded, having heard it the week before.

On Tuesday it did speak, and so I dropped
A glance at my own feet, for safety's sake;
And saw where the left one lifted up and stepped
Across a lighted depth which offered me
(The only passenger leaving for the street)
First option on its bright infinity . . .
I took my time — it was my time to take

And no one else's after all — and thought:
Those footlight bulbs shining beneath this train
Cry out for a performance. Therefore I brought
My right foot over, at the same leaden rate,
With sweating grace and flourish to complete
A great dramatic solo, of the sort
You don't need help with;
                though I'll appreciate

Company when I use that stop again.

Three Places

In the first I thought I was assuming
The substance of air and it was easy.
I was breaking into atoms and I was smiling.
I couldn't tell if they had given me
A room for this without or with a window,
I was facing a wall and couldn't turn round.
I was turning into air, and could make a sound
With my lips or in my throat; but who would know?

In the second I was somewhere on my back,
But recovered enough to realise it was a shelf,
And I was an object displayed on it. And a crack
Of rectangular light showed me my self
As a thing which might, at a nod or sigh,
Be shuffled into one piece and slid away
Into whatever slot of night or day
Was available to store or burn me in.

In the third it's different. Because I am whole
And moving at last — up a steep green
Corridor at the end of which my goal
Is a roomful of windows, and set between
The windows, chairs; and no flat shelves where I
Could watch my self spread out. If I find the strength
In my hollow shell, I'll climb the length
Of this polished cliff. And sit to watch the sky.

Exercise

When I suddenly made out I was near to the edge,
I could balance still, and not shake or shiver,
But I couldn't tell with mind or hand or foot
How near it was; or for that matter
If what I took for the brink was in fact the brink;
Or on the other hand whether
An opening-out of the sky around me
Made it *seem* like the brink.

And naturally I knew this was all pretend,
But I couldn't remember how many or how few
Imagined yards I'd left before I would take
One step too many, and fall down over or through
Crash and finish the game.
I had to be sure it was true
That the path behind could lead me down again.
I had to find voice enough to *Stop the Game!*

Repairs

On Monday the scaffolding went down
Like propelling pencil leads
On the rough cloth of the lawn.

On Tuesday it went up like a framework
Of medical attention round the house.
A water-hose dripped nourishment on the bricks.

Today I feel retained inside it
Like a structure too piecemeal, too frail
To stand up by itself.

I need to believe it was worth all
Their fixing in place of tubes and bolts
And planks and pulleys, that everything

Will be better for the work than it was before.
They come to dismantle it to-morrow.
I need to believe I shall still be here.

Back

So whose are those postcards, typewriters, sunglasses?
And who piled some last-year's newspapers like that,
Not thinking that he might not be coming back?

To move through such belongings as one alive
And feel I am a dead man who left them just
As they are lying now, seems ridiculous . . .

But why doesn't the sun on the table give my hand
A shadow when it riffles these letters, which
Are all addressed to him? And when I look,

It ought to give my whole body a shadow too.
I should understand why the shapes of all these objects
Are so clear they shine; but I don't. Could it be because

I am crying at them? Otherwise, how explain
The ridiculous optical delusion of
My shadow suddenly slanting out from somewhere

And claiming them for its inheritance?

Spring Sonnet

A spring twilight, and nothing happening.
It's not getting darker and each garden tree
Looks painted against a silent gathering
Of clouds fixed cleanly into a bigger
Frame of unearthly immobility.
I think it might be unlucky to step through
Into so frozen and so mild a scene,
Where nothing grows or changes; it might give
The signal for all those images to move
And resume their earthly malice. Besides, down there
To the right, next to the hedge, a bent wax figure
With his arms clamped onto a handle and his two
Painted lips fixed into a frozen stare,
Is waiting to start up the wind-machine.

Inertia Reel

Waking after the nightmare of a too-high urinal

Dawn: a new day waiting, terrified, to be auditioned

I shave, forgetting I have a beard. I dress, not remembering I meant to slop around in pyjamas. I have a super ego, but is its memory going?

First Steps in Hypochondria (a Correspondence Course)

Ah, a brisk morning walk! Feeling good, but a bit like a newly-sharpened pencil: a little less left than yesterday

And no real appetite for lunch. I'm offered another nymphet but I'm full up already

Hypochondria Lesson Three: not the strength in your fourth toe you had at forty

Eat All You Want and Still Look Anorexic (a Correspondence Course)

So the afternoon stretches insensibly on, past the hour of my birth in a climatic and economic depression

And tea-time already! Not ready for it, nostalgic about lunch, the oilcloth on the table, the glass cruet won at hoop-la, the savoury mince

In the newspaper: Barnacles make trusty pets

Hypochondria Lesson Eight: Never stir weak tea, let your toast cool a little, *always* boil lettuce before eating

Sunset: rehearsal for what might just come right *to-morrow* evening

Send for your barnacle today (meaning: Pay us to unload our vagrant crustacea on *you*)

How to relate to your bedclothes (a Correspondence Course)

In the newspaper: Scientists have proved that the time we spend asleep thinking we are awake and the time awake thinking we are asleep cancel each other out

Last thought at night before sleep overcomes my dread of it: Oh, I shall survive; but it will take a second lifetime

Over the Road

With a hand held to her face after the dentist,
The woman has crossed the carriageway towards
A known-to-be-sympathetic long-haired cat;
The pain is over and the two are smiling.

The tall man wearing pressed corduroys
Has crossed behind her with the jaunty pace
Of a reassured lover, so he too survives
A very high statistical risk:

There is more black death on the M25
Than there was in Surrey in 1349.
The Basra Road is safer than Oxford Street.
It is safer to cross the Atlantic than Belsize Park.

I am half across, and stand in the draught
Of an island left between two deathly streams.
I rest my hand on a bollard, no protection,
And the venerable rust of antiquity stains me,

But I stand and breathe, in the unforeseen sunlight,
In one of those minutes when nothing can touch me,
As certainly as the woman and the cat
Can touch each other and the man stride on.

There's a feel of new leases being taken out.

Sixtieth

The way those waves are processing
Towards me this afternoon, their ceremonial
    Sets of uncurling crests . . . Is the sea attempting
Some sort of tedious message? It seems that all
    It offers is some maxim like *To me*
All things must return or *Watch this space*
    Which opens for you — so enticingly:
You're bound to enter it and feel at ease . . .

Is it ever going to halt those blue
Monotonous arrivals? From where I stand,
    Half-a-mile away, is it trying to wash through
The tops of that rim of pine trees, where the land
    Makes one final gesture, and the heath declines
Down into the dunes? There's a village on the left,
    And some ploughland slopes off up some contour lines
To the right, and a slow, persistent, deft

And ritual patience of the sea licks, licks at
This whole scene, starting with the trees — in vain,
    As if it's lost its touch. I'm thinking that
I have no time at all now for its plain
    Repetitions of the old siren pledge
To win and keep me.
                        Though the whole long day
    Is setting with that sun, each field and hedge
Looks green and living still, as I stride away.

19

II

Incident in 1912

The boy, an only child, is taken out
To tea with some cousins. They are a family
Of five exuberant girls; and they dance and shout
In the absolute conviction that you are better
For being five than if you are merely one.
To be a singleton can't be much fun,
So the five of them dance round him mockingly;
And in forty years' time all six receive a letter.

Forty years later, somebody will write
With news for all of these people; but that can wait.
The boy wears a brand-new sailor-suit, the spite
Of the five capering cousins is taken out
On its trim blue smartness: one of them dips a spoon
In the gooseberry jam-pot, and very soon
His trousers are smeared with pips, and a huge great
Blob runs down his collar, all this without

Any protest from their mother, the boy's aunt,
Who is used to such behaviour in her brood
(How can you punish every jape and taunt?)
But upright on the upright piano stands
A sepia photograph of Aunt Caroline,
Indomitable, single and fifty-nine,
Who knows how these girls will not come to much good,
And that the devil finds work for idle hands.

In minutes the boy is close to resentful tears,
He retreats into a corner, the girls pursue;
Aunt Caroline lives on for forty years,
Or, to be precise, she dies at ninety-six.
His parents are enraged, but his mother won't
Presume or dare to utter the word *Don't*
To her sister's children. Aunt Caroline, too,
Would simply watch and ponder these bullying tricks

If she were there. Back home, the stricken boy
Vows never to go back, never to speak, at all,
To these cousins, who so thoroughly enjoy
Being five in the family that they must ridicule
Less fortunate children. Aunt Caroline is poor,
And thrifty; and behind her bedroom door
Has a mirror, fitted loosely to the wall,
Where she stores unspent pound notes. The space is full

By the time she dies, she has had few bills to pay,
So the sum went on increasing. Other hands
Came to count it in the end, hands that knew the way
The law must apportion each intestate pound;
And eventually the solicitor's tidings drop
Onto various family doormats. At the top
The letter says: *In re Miss Caroline Sands,*
Deceased: We beg to inform you we have found

The estate of the above to be valued, net,
At two thousand pounds, most of it cash concealed
At 94, The Crescent. If you kindly let
Us know the names of those to receive due shares
We should be much obliged. The angry boy
Is a married man today; and he learns with joy
The import of this letter, which has revealed
A most amazing justice; and who cares

That he was mocked, nearly forty years ago,
By that spiteful mob for being an only child!
Each branch of this cousinhood will soon know
What share of the two thousand to expect,
And in one large and noisy family,
When they see that the cash will be shared out equally
Between branches, not individuals, a wild
Delight will change to curses. 'Is this a fact,'

One girl exclaims, 'that because I am one of five,
I receive only sixty pounds of this hidden hoard,
While in the post for that one child will arrive

24

A letter and a cheque for over three
Hundred quid? It isn't fair, it's a disgrace!
That stupid boy, with green jam on his face,
Will be getting five times my share? This is absurd.
We'll write to this solicitor instantly . . .'

But next day she 'phones the boy, to say that she'd
Love to see him, with her sisters, to celebrate . . .

* * *

The boy remembers the last time, and is afraid.
Their mockery still hurts him, and the lack
Of kindness in people. Still . . .

                         Though he made that vow
Not to visit them ever again, well *now*
– *No!* He cannot change his mind. It's much too late.
They are planning some strange revenge . . . He will not go back.

Neglected Fire

My mother says, *That bonfire's still alight,*
But I can't tell where she's pointing. *On the right,*
Can't you see it now?
                                And then I catch one spark
At the far end by the plane tree, in a dark
Recess of the undertrimmed garden where
She does sometimes light fires. So I lean and stare
Through the room the light paints on the window pane
As she holds back the lace curtain, and some rain
– Or sleet, or snow – blurs the garden with sharp spots
Drumming down on the glass. And I shift some pots
On the unsteady scullery table, hoping for
A clearer view as she moves off through the door:
I can't have raked it over properly,
She murmurs guiltily; to herself not me.

But though they went on creeping back into
Our after-supper talk in the room we knew
As 'the kitchen', no one ever thought to go
And make the fires safe; our pre-war radio
Detained us, with its post-war comedies.
While out there in the garden, under the trees,
The flames were obstinately burning on,
My mother was reminding us that one
Small spark could fire a city, she had no doubt
That someone should have gone and stamped them out;
And all loose ends were living wires, they'd kill
If you forgot, and touched them.
                                But with no will
To act herself she left us reassured
That most fires died out of their own accord.

Lost

Would they play it on the wireless if we asked?
Would they know it? Would they have it in the archives?
Would they think it worth playing a lost old tune?
Aren't we too old to ask? Aren't they too young to see the point?

The scarred and scratched, the rutted, bakelite
Of a million 78s around the world,
Reduced to a nostalgic cackle-crackle,
Its voices out of pre-electric time,
Is everywhere waiting requests from the nearly dead:
Can't you play something for us?
Having come so far we are immutable now,
We are going to stay immutable until death,
And we'd love to hear that lost old tune again.
Can't you play it for us, on the very last gramophone
Equipped to play 78s?

A girl went down to the actually dead
To enquire about her lost virginity:
The dead are a great Lost Property Office
From which no postcards about things handed in
Are ever mailed out. But the girl went down
Because there are more virgins even now
Than there are ex-virgins among the dead,
And she believed such girls might have an answer.

When she came back up she was still an ex-virgin,
But she carried in her hands some precious discs
The dead had given her, made of bakelite
— There are things the dead will yield up if the living
Go and ask them with a genuine respect.
'Give them those,' the dead had said, 'and they can put them
In their archives to be played when they get requests,
When they get those enquiries after the lost old tunes

From those who remember, or have read about,
The innocence of popular music, lost
Midway between the Somme and the Wall Street crash.'

Anniversaries

With the old pre-electric telephones
The crackle was louder,
The scraping of cosmic sandpaper more violent.
When your voice came through from Yucatan
It sounded authentic; for months
I hoarded your tiny atmospheric phrases.
I like to believe you hoarded mine
Like the last shilling in the tin.

Now that you come through every day,
And you're almost 'in the room',
I don't credit one clear breathing word;
After an hour has passed I remember
Virtually nothing. Unless
They give us that sandpaper back again,
I'll imagine you spending me in Yucatan
Like the last million in the tin.

Not Known

Somehow you left us out of your address books.
If we suddenly became important, then
You would have no way of finding us except
Through some small clear memories; you might conclude
We were irretrievably distant, as good as dead
After such long silence. But though you hardly
Think of us, we think about you; and be assured
We are here when you want to recall us, always willing
To return and be known again.
                              Yes, properly known
For the first time ever . . . You should get in touch.
We are living at the bus routes' farthest ends,
Collecting box-number mail about once a month,
And waiting alive to be traced by teams of searchers:
As soon as you decide, they can drive fast
Along empty roads in their TA 21s,
And bring us back again, preserved and clean
In the black-and-white photography of your past.

Two Prospects of Adolescence

(i)

My shoes left neatly side by side alone,
My socks peeled down and draped over a rock,
My trousers rolled in even folds, each fold
(As I was always taught it ought to be)
The exact breadth of a turn-up . . .

I kept them all in sight from the shoreline,
Where I steadied myself on the sand's hard corrugations
And confronted the North Sea with my book.
The wind felt at my feet and at my shin-hairs
As I waited for the sea to catch me up . . .

And I stood it out in ankle-deep ripples, reading
Of the party that echoed in Auerbach's cellar,
And Gretchen growing in the dreams of Faust;
While my friends, up in the dunes, trembled in trances
That dared the flagrance of lovers in Pompeii . . .

(ii)

I am remembering by re-reading you:
We are dancing together over my diary's page,
And we are dangerously breakable!
Oh we would shatter into ruins if
We went any closer, the polite and maladroit boy
And the circling girl . . .

                It's late, I close the book
On my squandering of all that innocence.
How it could have prepared me . . . Why did I never see
That the fear and inexperience provided
Premonitions of a truth it took so much
More living to recognise: all there ever was
Was breaking?
            I am longing in the dark

To recover the feel of those intact gyrations,
Your fingers resting on my shoulder and scarcely
Touching it, my right hand at your waist,
My left hand neat in your clammy and clean hand.

Old Scene

Merchants trade spices in the shadow of
The emperor's new fortress. From above,

A guard looks down, and watches prisoners pass
In bored long lines across the imperial grass

Towards the mindless toil of the plantations.
Their footfalls stir the fortress's foundations,

And the walls begin to tremble. In time, in years,
The stones work loose, the fortress disappears,

And we have romantic ruins, just one tall door
-way opening onto desert . . . From his store

Selling drinks and gifts, the guard looks out, he sees
The tourists pass in listless companies

On their way back to the coaches (a merchant goes
To his camels to unload his videos).

They toil at coloured postcards on the way
Back to the Sheraton Hotel; and another day

Is over, on the same old scene night falls,
At leisure, on the hotel's fortress walls.

Lucky Thirteen

Don't call, just come. Come into the room,
Hang your shirt over the mirror and 'feel free'.
I put the telephone down in that corner,
Underneath my nightdress. The air-conditioning?
Noisy, probably safe; but I'll play some rock.
Sit down in one chair and hold conversation
To start. Any more, *write it down, write it down*!
. . . Prepare yourself to wake quickly if you sleep,
And I hope you not talk in your sleep.
From here you will see the sun rise over
The Heroes' Monument. If it does,
And you stay long enough for that, it will be
The first times we ever kiss in daylight.

A Walk by Moonlight

I cross the side of the Square at a safe walk,
And shall soon be passing the solitary guard
At the Palace. Up beyond him, one in a dark
Leather jacket stands; and waits. I am assured
By his noncommittal look that I have been seen.
This is ten seconds after nine-thirteen.

Keeping to one of the two permitted routes,
I am thirty yards from where he leans on the tall
Palace railings, when he devalues his cigarettes
By lighting one. TRAIASCA PARTIDUL
COMUNIST ROMAN, say the letters of the sign
On the Central Committee, opposite. Two lights shine

From its huge grey rectangle. One is a bright
Slant of yellow from the door, which strangely stands
Wide open, and the second is a late
Lamp lit in a fourth-storey window, a light which sends
The message that Someone is working up there,
At nine-fifteen above Republic Square!

And are they suspicious of me, walking up
The pavement towards them? Because the man
Now approaches the soldier (whose trained grip
Doesn't slacken for a second on his gun) . . .
Could it be that I become the subject of
The muttered conversation these two have?

Now I've passed, but their faces are still watching the only one
To disturb them for some while; and though their voices
Talk freely, they still talk quietly. When I look in
-to the clockmakers' window I see other faces
Saying it's nine-sixteen and all is well.
I'm two minutes away from the hotel.

* * *

Now that I'm back I have enjoyed my outing.
The clerk at the desk is ready with my key.
When I enter the lift, which has been waiting
While I've been out, I get its night and day
Rattle of muzak; and I hope the door
Will open, at the hush of the fourth floor.

Yes, my shirt hangs on the mirror, where it was,
And my notepad hasn't moved. On the counterpane
Are my dictionary and tablets.
                              I'll watch the news
With *Telejurnal*; after which the screen
Will give me the Inspector, the good Roman,
To-night, and no doubt for some nights to come . . .

* * *

If anyone is listening, I'm at home.

                                        Bucharest 1987

Experience near Porlock

A cry, a crash, and a vengeful shout
From the street below; and I have written:
The mountains had to start somewhere, so why not
Immediately rising out of flat fields
Where the sheep need no stamina for grazing?
I saw them do this from the train on Thursday;
And the next afternoon I saw from a window
The train I travelled on the day before
As it wormed across my picture without me,
A pleasantly far-off giant insect.
I watched it, it used up no stamina
When I grazed on it, so I slipped myself back
Inside it, and dreamed I still travelled as I lay
On the grass of a foothill under the mountains
The day after that, the day which was yesterday.
I could see the train from there as well, see the window
From which I saw the train, and from that third place
The two were in a calmly vanishing past
I was dying to hold on to. — But then came today,
With an evening too dark to see very much at all,
Only dream about it in the vanishing
Room behind the window; and only write
A drunk has finished the dreams in his bottle
And smashed it to bits on the pavement.

Mark and Melinda
Prepare the Luggage

You two, please take us back now we understand.
Take us back now we speak the language more like our own.
Take us back now our questions aren't simple-minded.
Take us back now we don't want just the phrasebook answers.

We didn't believe in you in your two dimensions,
We might believe in you now you've grown the third.
Let's all take a plane to where life is so much freer,
Where there'll be a little restaurant we can't speak

For the thump of the rock band, and as we leave
We'll be ordered to enjoy our days, some place
Where the crucifixes advertise Coca-Cola.
— Perhaps we'll take a plane to Budapest

So Mark can stand again on the Erzsébet Bridge
In the fumes of the traffic he taught us the words for
When there wasn't much of it; and stroll round the boutiques
Behind the Lenin Boulevard that was.

And Melinda, let's go back to Keleti Station,
Buy some tickets at the window, stand and punch them
In the little machine on the wall of the yellow tram
Past the cemetery where János Kadar lies,

Past the flat where József Antall is living now.

January to April

So we've come through, to a cold plain stretch
Without commitments; and might as well
Go for new beginnings because there's nothing much
To do except begin. Besides, this spell
Of shining January sunsets looks as clear
As our first, clean diary pages of the year

. . . Except that the prospect is suddenly stained
By a squire with a shotgun, warning me to keep
My nose out of his business. Beyond him stand
His shooting party, angry and kneedeep
In root-crops blasted by frosts; from near and far
They glower in fury at my intruding car

For giving out a warning to the prey
Their beaters wanted to scare up from the ground.
Their attitudes suggest a wasted day,
And their smiles are threatening: I feel I've found
Where the heart of England beats to fortify
Its old solid bones and veins, and I can't deny

That I'm pleased to have upset a project whose business
Was impersonal slaughter; though it manages
Few corpses today, and they like me even less
On account of that. To-night, strange images
Of death, by remote control, will fill their screens,
And armchair switches bring them warmer scenes . . .

This February is mild, and yet last night
The temperature fell, and further cattle-stuff
Was ruined. In its longer, colder light
There's no one to intercept me if I make off
Down the same track today, through fragile snow
Where mud and guns delayed me weeks ago.

The squire has gone, leaving the game to me,
And my walk is a way of meditating on
The questions left behind by his memory:
Is mankind worse with the missile than the gun?
Does it work more evil with remote control?
And at how many removes will the whole

Moral issue vanish completely? Farther on,
A hare sprints across my path, turns round and looks,
And waits like a dog, a prey for anyone . . .
I could teach it to be moral and read books
As fast as I could teach the squire's young friends
Not to fire if they saw it. When the short month ends

And March arrives, the winter still holds out.
It's the worst time, flaunting every day the dream
Of a spring which it denies. Yet who can doubt
That its coming will seem banal? New girls will scream
With the old enjoyments, while their elders sit
And give up trying to make sense of it

— Someone tell them it's all useless, that the world will
Never change, merely pass through frost and blood
From the snowdrop to the ridiculous daffodil
Every year; pushing flowers up through the mud
Of death's green season from a hope which tries
To appease the bones and the smashed weaponries . . .

And where the daffodil surfaces again
In the squire's fields, and demands some celebration,
I stop my car today in the April rain,
And see it only as a distillation
Of the palest hope earth could ever seek and find
In a war which left so few whole bones behind . . .

1991

In Moslodina

'If we never learn much from history it is because
"we" are always different people.'

In the Tourist Hotel somebody leaves a tap
Running too long. The first drip to fall on me
Strikes at my left thigh; the second stays
Poised over the armchair, then suddenly
Runs, and drops several inches farther up;
The third and fourth I catch in two ashtrays.

Forgetting my own bath, I rush to get
Dressed and raise Cain, cursing a world with too
Many forgetful fools in it, and surely far
More than there used to be? Plus, a huge new
Tribe of the unknowing, happy to let
Some others tell them what their memories are.

The drips fill tumblers, vases. Through the dead
Door of the room upstairs a national song
Booms to drown my knocking. Girls in folkloric dress
Light candles on T.V. . . . I watch a long
Dark, cross-shaped patch on the ceiling form, and spread:
A continent of sheer forgetfulness.

The Girl in the Booth

When she has taken our money inside
Her wooden box, she begins to talk and shout
Above the music nobody thinks about,
Above the roar of the floor where our dodgems ride
Round and round unaware of the repeated
Laugh, laugh from the Haunted House. She stares, and grips
A microphone with one hand, and her puppet lips
Mouth her message in a dull, defeated
Monotone: You are no more than crippled birds
Fallen into the lights and left to blunder through
Ten last minutes of life. And is it true
That you think it's *freedom*? – No one can hear her words.

Entering my Sixty-second Year

I've always had this dread of growing old
In untidiness: a worn tobacco pouch;
The edges of a table cloth rubbed and frayed
Into tassles; accumulators; a deep drawer
Full of tram maps and busted pipes; a couch
Where a dusty cushion pictures an esplanade
In faded Devon; all my grandfather's store.
Long after he was dead and his goods were sold

(But mostly chucked away) those hoarded treasures
Seemed what it meant to live on to his age,
And I, too, would end with the same cruel
And pointless load of close-at-hand bric-a-brac
Stuck round *me*, like the toys fixed in the cage
Of a tamed songbird. Dud capsules of lighter fuel,
Old tins, ancient Pelicans, today brings back
The dread-full sight of them, an old man's pleasures

(And his failures) — I can feel his presence
In the junk in my own room. So now I'm able
To picture myself his age, I'll up and set
The VCR, spread brand-new books among
The dustless disks on my working-table,
And fight back with Order; hoping to forget
That because this is my life, my style, the young
May see it as my trash, my obsolescence.

The White Lady
in memoriam George MacBeth

I found your door, and touched your bell
  The same day my friend died.
I said, 'I've come to buy your love
  Because I'm terrified.'

The terror was of death itself,
  For his, and my own sake;
Whoever knows how much more love
  One faltering heart can take?

— And terror, too, at what I'd done
  By taxi-ing to you,
When sorrowing for a dead man was
  The tribute that seemed due.

I grieved for one whom my friend loved,
  The last who understood
Words were his blood and sinews but
  Her body was his food . . .

Had I dredged up some craven lust
  From younger, darker years
To smother up with sweat and sperm
  A night that called for tears?

But — 'You make love to me,' I said,
  'My friend has died, and rests,
A shrunken thing, in wasted bones . . .
  I'll pay you for your breasts,

'And lips, and hairs, and supple hands,
  And tongue that raises me
And licks away the feel of death's
  Putrescent infamy.'

You said, 'You pay me for my tits
    And my hands to work you mad,
And, like, I'll pay you back your friend
    With things would make him glad

'If he could know you cried for him
    So hard you came to find
A girl to rub away the ash
    That settled on your mind.'

And you, blonde stranger, knelt your nine-
    teen years above my pain,
And crying with me paid me back
    My old friend's life again

— Because, I crept back to my room,
    Your softly-punished child,
And in last summer's photographs
    I *swear* he knew; and smiled.

III

The Telescope

But these days, like gazing down it the wrong way:
Thus, a hotel corridor focuses a street
Where a hub-cap fills most of a small door
With an aluminium circle, as complete
As a big ship constructed in a yard; which looms
To block the sky above the dying town
That built it. The row of shops and curtained rooms
Is blocked out by this container, soon launching down
To the seas of a One Way system; but now two
White-bloused and black-haired visions cross the floor
Halfway down the passage, and start a new,
A likelier flash of interest . . . I can't stay

— And I'm leaning on a long cylinder of straw
An hour later, someone's machine-made feed
For the winter; it pierces through my shirt
And stirs my skin. That onward track must lead
To the sea, though first there's a restful skyline
With a soft swell of wheat on it . . . I watch
A dragonfly drop and settle, and define
The colour blue on a grey stony patch
Of the path, where one journey of tractor wheels
Has laid two ruts, suggesting a harm and hurt
Which feet don't inflict. And very soon this feels
Like a place where you can't be exactly sure

How you ever came. So I move on, still in hope
Of finding the sea; until at last I stand
By the edge of a tidal lake from where I see
Over there a metal sign stuck in the sand,
Forbidding something — though whatever its intent,
It seems to be saluting the marching skin
Of the water, a parade of ripples sent
Forward, forward by the afternoon breeze in
Perpetual advance to a climax somewhere,
Some high point of ocean . . . Attainably

Close, would you think? Like the breast of wheat? Like the hair
Of the girls who walked in the tiny telescope?

The Advantages of Small Town Life

Where the cultivation of sameness is the law,
A variant sub-clause like you can provide
The difference everybody can enjoy.
It's fame to be a bedtime conversation
In three thousand five hundred blue heavens.

You have curious little habits they chat about,
And encourage: a barman's right hand
Goes up to the grenadine when you enter their pub,
His left to the worcester sauce. Your green moustache
Is charisma in ten thousand memories.

You're an amiable chap, and such a deep one!
Most of your telephone calls are from ministers,
The operators say so; your light's on late
And a rumour spreads: He's at work on a scheme
For harnessing the force of unwanted erections.

Your presence is power, your absence is power,
Your unexpected return is a thunderbolt.
They know about your postcards from Novi Sad.
With a daily walk they can time things by,
You can miss out once, and their eggs will be boiled to brick.

For years you can cash their illusions about you
For the D-marks of licence. To be different means
To feel envied, to feel free, they are less than you,
You are noticed everywhere. And at any time
Their deputation with Tsornoffs will know where to find you.

Principal Boy

At her very first entrance she outshines   All the sycophants
    and spivs   She strides with tall ease on a stage that
    looks manageable now   Its agoraphobic wastes seem
    amenable to reason

We see there's a bold young man to the rescue who is
    also   A daring resourceful girl   She can act like a
    tough brave boy and be dashing and strong   But will
    never never surely be loutish or rough

So she's Brother and Sister at once and can   Remember the little
    things and be Mother as well   But she's handsome
    Brother entirely courting the Princess   And for all of
    the time whenever she speaks and sings

Her role is supposed to have nothing to do with sex   You
    may only purely admire her no other emotion   It is
    not to be even a distant aseptic love   You could
    never forget a kiss and yet never desire her

If a sultan or vizier shouts or a genie shows bottle   She
    looks scared like a woman but that is only
    pretence   She's gallant and good in every turmoil or
    scrape   It's just that she doesn't want to seem
    superhuman

Supremely she disentangles the threads in all the plotting   If
    there's villainy in the way she propels it aside   We
    walk with her unharmed through the thickets of
    childhood fear   We always knew she was destined to
    win the day

And then at last yes the walls lift and fold back and she
    shows us   The hills and the sun when the whole dim
    scene is transformed   She is puffing us up for the
    world outside the Exits   Where we have to face up to
    the Fact That Life Has Begun

We remember and worship her legs in the homegoing
        tram   She is out there imperishable somewhere in the
        dark   She is watching and waving and smiling and
        saying   'Be strong! Shall you look on my works you
        meek ones and despair?'

A Dark Blue Day

I have to call it something like despair,
Forgetting the name of somebody who came
Across a room and very suddenly
Set herself down in an opposite chair
And placed her two stockinged feet on the arm
Of my own chair at twenty-five past three

Thirty years ago! Because, I could tell she guessed
No one else would be watching, the window only showed
The rooftops and part of the sky, which we could see
Had turned a dark blue, darker than the rest,
And I missed the chance she offered . . . I recall it snowed,
With the flakes failing to settle, just timidly

Wafting over the brickwork of the grey
Terraced streets which rose up slowly from the river
Like an adjunct of its mist. – And I think I know
That the town could be found once more, that dark blue day
And those grey streets reappear, if I could ever
Call up her name; which would persuade the snow

To fall again, and the room to still be there
With its window onto rooftops, and cloudy light
Shining into a narrow space where two people meet
Thirty years ago, each stuck in a deep armchair
Pretending to guess if the snow might fall all night
– And the man would settle for stroking the woman's feet.

February

Once there was half-term, now it's only
Four pale little lunar weeks without a focus:
Days to tread water in, fill the pending tray
Of an ante-room month, and gather weeds
For the obsequies of the Old Financial Year.

I have heard old wise men in the country say,
'But there's always one day the sun'll give you
A hint of spring in the middle of February!'
— Wrong as usual. I shall relax and enjoy it
In the inevitable wake of winter.
You tell me that the days are drawing out?
Like freezing poultices.

To Delay

for Stephen Spender

The searching for empty seats
The listening hard to announcements
The skitter of electronic signboards
Through place and place and place
The re-reading of paperbacks
The purchase of useless gifts
The faces masked with boredom
Wired into walkmen
In the rip-off bars

— And the consequent need
For long explanations
For cancelling rests
And abrupting meals
And ending shorter encounters
With briefer kisses
And using up limited time
In moving on fast to the next things
Much too rapidly done

— But sooner that than being left alone
At the very end when everyone else has gone
With their baggage and passports and children
All checked and accounted for
And too many seats to choose from
The overpriced restaurant shut
The sweeper's broom at your ankles
The public address switched off
The signboards finally blank

Bastard

Into a suddenly sunny spring dawn
A bastard creeps out through a crack in some
Until-then immaculate-looking woodwork.

He inhales the air and smiles, and everything
Looks good to him. And so he takes a few
Experimental paces, trying out

His legs and wondering what clothes to wear:
A city suit? Some jeans and a baseball cap?
Or an 'I ♡ my building society' T-shirt?

Because he plans to walk into an Organisation,
To stir things up inside an Organisation.
He is going to Go For It and get others Going,

And he's past Reception already, and up
In an express lift to a penthouse suite already,
And they have an office waiting for him already,

And his first dictated letters on a screen.
In the other offices, behind their hands,
They are talking about him, quite a lot,

They are saying, 'How did that bastard get that job?
I'd like to know where the hell he came from!
I'd like to see his qualifications for doing

What he does.' — All talk, and he knows it, it's safer
To talk than to act, the smaller bastards
Know the truth of that from long experience,

They've learnt to carry on and keep their heads down
To protect their own bit of woodwork.
                                    So all goes well,
With the faxes slithering out from other bastards

In other penthouse suites all round the world,
And the graph turning upwards on the wall-chart in
The Bastard's Conference Room, the spread-sheets glowing

With the marvellous figures the Bastard envisages;
And his desk is clear and shiny, and people's smiles
Are amiable and innocent, or seem so.

Or seem so . . . In his deep suspicious brain
The Bastard worries occasionally that their lips
May be smiling, smiling for him, but not their eyes.

Still, for now, things go splendidly, the Bastard is seen
On 'State of the Art' and 'Man of the Week', and has
A 'Room of my Own' and a 'Holiday of my Choice'.

— And then one day a casual conversation
Stops short when he enters a room without warning
And another day the people do not stop

When he comes round the door, but self-consciously keep
            talking
With knowing looks, and ever-widening smiles.
The Bastard pretends he hasn't noticed, but

He goes back to his office and he thinks
'Those bastards could be ganging up on me . . .
I must watch that little bastard with the haircut.'

The Bastard is full of fear and fantasy,
And the fantasy that made his world for him
Becomes a fantastic fear of losing it:

His mirror tells him always to guard his flanks,
And never leave his knife-drawer open when
He turns his back on even his secretary

– But he does have courage. It tells him to have it out
Face-to-face with his team of Assistant Bastards
And find out what the hell is going on.

Oh no, they'll never tell him half the story,
Oh yes, they'll sit and talk behind their hands,
But he can still fire the lot; or he thinks he can.

Today they are gathered round a table, with vellum pads
Which some of them are writing or doodling on,
And some are self-confidently leaving quite untouched.

It's the ones who pick up no pencils and take no
Notes who are the most dangerous. They know
The result they want without fidgeting about it;

Especially the little bastard with the haircut.
He speaks in code but it's clear what he's implying:
The Bastard is letting the Organisation down,

It ought to do better; and all the smallest bastards,
The shareholders' democracy, have been stirred
To demand a different bastard at the top.

This year they're eager for a different scene,
This year they're after a man with a different style,
This year they'd like a bastard with a haircut.

The Bastard's hand is turning clammy on
His thoroughly doodled vellum pad,
The sky is blue for other bastards now.

He sees what is coming next, and he'll speak out first.
He rises from the table, he looks at them
With steady eyes, and steady eyes look back,

Though the lips are smiling. 'I've seen your game!' he shouts,
'I've sussed it out – you're just a lot of *bastards*,
A lot of dirty, crooked, scheming *bastards*!'

When the door slams hard behind him they look at each other
And shake their heads with humane and pitying smiles.
'Poor bastard,' one compassionately murmurs.

The haircut says, 'It wasn't easy, but
It had to be.' And a third: 'I'm so relieved
It's over and we can breathe.' And a grinning fourth

In a flak jacket moves into the Bastard's chair
As the sun sets golden, and the immaculate walls
Begin to look like very porous woodwork.

Adlestrop Now

The name, as I drove west that day,
Flashed from a hedgerow. Since the sign showed
Only two miles, having time enough
I took the little winding road

Along to the village. First I passed
A wood, and then a field where straw
Burnt black, and near a notice-board
Which said 'Neighbourhood Watch', I saw

Two well-trained citizens staring hard
At me, and at my number-plate.
Alarms clung to cottage walls, and locks
Guarded each wild-rose porch and gate,

And after a brief stay, I thought
I'd go. I had no wish to stir
Rumour in all those covered nests
Of Oxfordshire and Gloucestershire.

Agents and Patients

When I sit taking an interest in people
(My little notebook hidden on my knee)
I often remark how little interest
People seem to take in me . . .
Would this merely suggest
That I manage to do it with a fair
Show of tact? Or don't they see me there at all?

Those two greybeards playing backgammon are
Bent over the desperate issues of the game,
Going bald in the pursuit of it — not because
My watching them is to blame
For driving them hairless
With paranoia. They are not even aware
There is anyone else in their Byzantine bar.

As for the woman in the crimson and green
Hat in the Lapland shop: Not to forget her,
I snatch a scrap of paper to write her down,
And it doesn't appear to upset her,
If she notices; her frown
Is for something else. — There is this large divide
In the world, as large as the gulf between

Rock-lovers and rational people: On one hand
The observers, on the other the oblivious
Objects of observation, guiltlessly eager
To sit down without fuss
And eat their *dal* or *mamaliga*;
And not need to eat any words, as the writer might
Who learns that the 'businessman' drumming his heel to the
      band

Is a linguistic philosopher from Keele.

Ballad Form Again

Seated one day in the sauna,
　　Hands on my steaming knees,
Counted my two feet, got it right,
　　Thought, What do I do with these?

Numbered my human failings,
　　Pardoned them one by one,
Took a shower and dried myself,
　　Walked out into the sun

— Snatched for my dark, dark glasses
　　Moment I hit the light;
Find shade a little easier,
　　Can't take the world too bright.

Strolled through the City Centre,
　　Followed the One Way signs
To the Consumer Precinct,
　　Saw the new clothes designs,

Saw the new architecture
　　In the new eclectic style:
Post-modern Bauhaus Gothic.
　　Looked at the gargoyles smil-

Ing on the old church pinnacles
　　As the sky turned grey then black,
Folded my dark, dark glasses,
　　Thought of turning back

But pressed on, with my umbrella,
　　As the hail began to pelt:
More climatic experience
　　Under my belt . . .

For shelter, was there a tea-room
   Or a library to be found?
No – only the hypermarkets
   Gleaming all around.

Trod carelessly in the gutter,
   Water gushed over me;
Thought, Forces of Nature as usual,
   Behaving amorally.

My feet being wet in my footwear,
   I decided to call it quits,
So I lowered my umbrella,
   Collected my few wits,

And checked the number of gargoyles
   – Thirteen vindictive elves!
Thought, Don't take the piss out of gargoyles,
   They do it for themselves.

Headed back home, determined
   Not to go out again
To waste the good of a sauna
   Walking in lousy rain.

Thought, Shoes which let in water
   Should be junked for sterner stuff;
And the same goes for the ballad form:
   Enough is enough.

In the Break

SAATCHI AND SAATCHI:
FIRST OVER THE WALL

– West Berlin
graffito, 1989

In the Amusement Arcade was a small glass case
Containing a wooden bird with a beak that smiled.
For a one-pound-coin you could turn a handle and
It flapped and flapped its coloured wooden wings.
This was like the freedom given to the East
To wear our coloured wings and flap for coins.

* * *

There are the black wings of death
That frighten us into living,
And there are the coloured wings of death
That brighten us into forgetting.

The flap of the first wings almost touches us.
Because they come to remind us we are mortal,
The moments we hear them we know we are still alive.
When we hear them passing over we know we are free.

But under the other, coloured wings of death
We hear and feel nothing to pain or alarm us:
They flatter and soothe and leave us unfree.
They would like us to believe they were wings of life.

They are wings of death which sing with the liberty
Of clockwork nightingales. They cool our skins
With air-conditioned breezes. They sing 'It is freedom
To choose us.' And they are leaving us unfree.

To say they do not matter is not to be free,
And to say 'I find them amusing' is not to be free,
And to watch them with a superior look but still
Stay watching is not to be free.

The black wings never change, you can recognise them
Always. But the coloured wings sometimes acquire
Transparency, they pose as natural,
Or they shift and alter like kaleidoscopes.

The black wings of death can never be defeated,
But you can do something about those coloured wings:
You can cut them by understanding what they are.
You can cut them with your indifference or your contempt.

You can cut them along the seams and through the stitches,
And tear them apart and let in the surrounding air;
Though to start this you need to be a bit free already,
Not a wooden bird yourself, flapping wings for money.

If you are free you will know where to find some scissors.

Sonnet of a Gentleman

How often have I courteously uncrossed
My legs to let someone in a tram pass by,
Only to kick him on the shins, thus lost
The whole point of the gesture! Some of my
Best efforts go for nothing . . . In a louts' age
A gentleman seems an anomaly,
Apt to incur bewilderment, even rage,
When his decency goes wrong.
                               But truthfully,
To be gracious, charming, courtly, open doors
For ladies, raise one's hat, use fountain-pens
Rather than biros — all this is a cause
Requiring no apologia or defence,
And in my heart of hearts I know I *am*
Helpful, and needed; like the city tram.

Vestibule Haiku

Ground.
> Plug, in an orange
> Socket, turns a tape. Girl clerks
> Proffer pens and smiles.

Mezzanine.
> Use-less hall space; glass
> Restaurant doors, sheets over
> The band's bright weapons.

First.
> Still you can't see sky.
> A Person from Porlock: *Am
> I disturbing you?*

Second.
> With signs, a 'Plan of
> Evacuation'. Useful!
> Blue plug-socket here.

Third.
> Miniature ferns
> In a chipped bowl; one glass door,
> Out of two, missing.

Fourth.
> Green ashtray grained like
> A breakwater. Carpets, clean.
> Laurel in a pot.

Fifth.
> Sky. A cloud looks through
> Lace drapes; lift-buttons bleached and
> Hollowed by fingers.

Sixth.
> Two old men in hats,
> Awkward with a lift arrived
> Too soon. Carpets? Stained.

Seventh.
> A wall clock wrenched out;
> A rose in a jar wilting
> Faster than its leaves.

Eighth.   The band-leader's room.
                   I know, seeing him go there
                       (All his summer life).

Ninth.   The last drone and gulp
                   Of the slow lift. I tread on
                       Carpets that fly air.

Roof Terrace.   What you feel, here you
                   Feel it: scared; free; bigger than
                       Tree, cart, ball, church, plums.

Incorrect

'Why must I pack and leave before noon today?'

'At Passport Control you used the ablative;
At Customs you opened your suitcase from left to right;
You summoned a taxi using the wrong fingers.
You did not pick up your key from the counter correctly
At Hotel Reception; you blinked in the lift; you did not
Remark on the arrangement of the bedside lamps.
Outside your window was a view of the marshalling yards
– You looked at it before teatime.
You went for a walk and did not pass the Statue;
Your failure to smile at them enough in the Gardens
Defamed the fun-hats of our Neo-Greens.
You went in to dinner promptly on the hour;
You dipped your spoon over-deeply in the soup;
You chewed the bread as if it was made of crumbs;
You cut your steak with unseemly emphasis;
You chose your dessert with unsuitable approval;
You sipped your coffee repeatedly moving your lips.
No doubt if we had watched you with greater attention
We would have found other rules infringed or neglected.
If we had monitored your mind when you slept,
We might have recorded inappropriate nightmares,
The wrong hobgoblins appearing in your dreams,
More shiftings of your blanket than were needed,
And a temptation to under- or oversleep
By numerous seconds.
                    Were you really not aware
Of any of these regulations before you came?
Did you not even trouble to open the Tourist Guide?
These are some of the reasons why you must leave by noon.
These are some of the reasons why you must never come back.'

'So what can I do, please tell me, to atone?
May none of these transgressions be forgiven?'

'You can do nothing. Things have gone too far. Besides,
Atonement has been abolished, and forgiveness
Is therefore redundant.

                    But – we make this clear –
Of course we shall be willing to overlook these crimes,
Of course we can permit you to stay as long as you wish,
Of course you may return whenever you like
– If you nod your head firmly, once, now. At the specified
        angle.'

Vladimir

Into the men's staff room of the second school
I taught in, in foggy nineteen fifty-five,
Through a term-ful of dripping days, with spiders' webs
Full of frost from October onwards on the bushes
In the gardens of the Council estate, would burst
At morning break, in drill suit, our P.E. man,
His whistle bouncing on his burly chest,
Shouting *Vladimir! My name is Vladimir*!
In a jarring deep bass voice I hate to think of
— That being a line recalled from a forgotten
B-feature film about Russian submarines
In the North Atlantic, threatening our liberty
To vote for Eden and commercial telly.
He'd fling the door wide open, bound in for coffee,
And boom out *Vladimir! My name is Vladimir!*
— Every bloody day. First we joined in, and then
It stopped being funny, and it never had been,
Though he kept it up well into January,
So giving himself a new nickname with the boys.

That same year, Mr, Sir, and (later) Lord
William Penney gave the world the British bomb,
On the Monte Bello islands; fall-out fell
Thirteen thousand miles away while our P.E. man
Felled fifteen maddened men with his stale joke
Which no one, from the start, had been amused by.
But — *Vladimir! My name is Vladimir!* . . .
If you could corner Plato — Aristotle —
Cicero — Thomas Aquinas — Goethe — Tolstoy —
And put it to them at some moment when,
Exhausted by high matters, they might *just*
Bend their minds to a small quixotic proposition,
I rather hope those sages might agree
That that man's joke (for which he got no knighthood,
No peerage either) had a slight moral edge
On what Lord Penney did, in that same year,

To keep fictitious Vladimir away;
And was a kinder gift to our mad world
Than all the cancers in the Indian Ocean.

Happiness near Sandefjord

The height-of-summer forests replete with surprise,
The very woodpeckers crying 'God bless our souls!'
— And our surprise, to burst out in the train
To the sunlight of a plain between rainclouds,
A space of streams and rocky villages
— And step down at the village where Herr Rasmusson
Took guests in a cabin bedroom beside the fields
On the Co-op gherkin farm he was manager of.

It was rain all night nevertheless,
But rain as one of the natural sounds
That partners any deep and healing silence,
And never infringes it. It drenched Herr Rasmusson's
Green lake of gherkin plants; but after breakfast
— Of sweet cold fish and onions and tomatoes
And crispbreads and butter and berry jam and coffee —
We sat and talked in English, discussed the gherkins

— And the sun came out! 'This is good, this is good,'
Said Herr Rasmusson. 'Now our chance to take the crop.'
'If it rain too big,' said Mrs Rasmusson,
'All the gherkins grow too fast, and in the wet
We cannot pick them, they grow into — "Marrows"?
The trucks that come to take them will *not* take them,
They are too big, no use collecting them
For the factory bottles.' 'Yes,' said Herr Rasmusson.

'If it rain too small, they not grow up enough
And we sit round lazy, my husband and myself,
My mother — "Mormor" — our son and all our workers,
We play draughts and wait.' 'Yes,' said Herr Rasmusson,
Looking out at the sun. And Mrs Rasmusson:
'The summer started dry, they were too small,
Now it rain too big, it never stop, we drown.'
'But it shine now,' said her husband, 'and we work. You too?'

74

We put on his recommended gloves because our hands
Would be grazed and torn by the plants, they could draw
          blood,
And we crossed the track to where the great leaves grew,
Sun-stained and -spotted, like huge maple leaves,
Cupping pure liquid ounces of rolling rain
That ran down in oily drops as you bent, and pushed
The undergrowth aside to get at the gherkins
On their prickly stalks of blotting-paper green.

You had to judge: If a gherkin was too large,
You plucked it all the same, but you threw it into
A separate bag for the uncollectables.
And if it was too small, and clung to its flower,
You left it to be picked in two days' time.
You looked for the happy medium, tried to see it
In a bottle of thirty in a downtown bar
– And carried it carefully to a wicker basket.

Where I crouched, the foliage swathed me, soaked my socks,
And my eagerness dragged the plants out of the soil
They had nearly grown out of anyway;
The best part was my cool, fastidious judgement.
When I stood, the sun hit me! Only we three
– My wife, young son and I – were exhausted already,
And easing our backs, a few dozen gherkins only
Having passed through our hands, strained and sore inside the
          gloves.

Herr Rasmusson, Mrs Rasmusson and Mormor,
And their workers old and young in Co-op sweatshirts,
Were away in a working line that had long outstripped us,
And were nearly up by then to the rocky horizon;
They had filled most of Mormor's woven baskets.
In about an hour we only filled one basket,
Though our cautious gherkins were all the proper size.
We stood and smiled, at a task only quarter-done.

We had tickets for the 11.10 to Oslo.
Herr Rasmusson came down from the top of the field:
'It is enough? You have done hard work for us,
You make many bottles!' His generous broad hand
Of thanks and leavetaking wore no protective glove,
His smiling jaw was stubbly with blond prickles.
We strolled away proud and happy in his praises,
Our own ungloved six hands all joined together.

— Except for our two outer hands, which lugged our cases.

Notes

A CORRIDOR (p. 9) – 'the store' (l.9) was Chiesman's in Lewisham High Street during my childhood and adolescence, currently (1994) a branch of the Army and Navy Stores chain, and differently set out. Going along the corridor of mirrors to the sports goods department where the ping-pong ball game was played was a frequent childhood walk. Later I could not understand why the game, which involved no skill, did not offend against gambling laws.

LOST (p. 27): l.34 – 1922, very roughly 'Midway between the Somme and the Wall Street crash' was when nationwide broadcasting began on a regularised basis in Britain, under the old 'British Broadcasting Company'. The wide distribution of popular music was destined eventually to remove its innocence in a way (the earliest) gramophone records had not.

NOT KNOWN (p. 30): l.15 – The Alvis TA21 was, in its day, the archetypally rapid and romantic motor vehicle, though the TA14 of 1948 was also capable of doing a ton.

A WALK BY MOONLIGHT (p. 35): l.10–11 – TRAIASCA PARTIDUL COMUNIST ROMAN: LONG LIVE THE ROMANIAN COMMUNIST PARTY. l.14 – Inspector Roman, a mildly Marxist cop, was the 'goodie' in a swashbuckling police series on Romanian television in the 1980s. Videos of it were a feature of hotel in-house transmissions.

JANUARY TO APRIL (p. 39) – It was the time of the Gulf War in 1991, the first war to be turned, not just partly (as with the Falklands conflict of 1982) but almost entirely into a video game relayed by the military to neutered journalists and a misinformed public.

IN MOSLODINA (p. 41) – I cannot recall the origin of the epigraph (a celebrated historian?), so may not have quoted the words exactly. 'Moslodina' is fictitious, but the poem's metaphor for the Bosnian horror presented itself when a bedroom ceiling actually did leak, for the reason described, in a Balkan hotel.

ENTERING MY SIXTY-SECOND YEAR (p 43): l.15 — It has surprised me that some people (and not just younger people) do not know about 'Pelicans' any more: the substantial light blue paperbacks of non-fiction (literature, history, politics, music) once published by Penguin.

THE WHITE LADY (p. 44) — An invention after the manner of certain poems by George MacBeth, written in homage to him the day after he died in 1992. (Incidentally, MacBeth rarely used them, but once jokingly professed himself 'very much in favour of leg-pulling notes at the end of slim volumes [of verse].')

THE ADVANTAGES OF SMALL TOWN LIFE (p. 51) — The Tsornoff firm supplied a wide range of military equipment to the armies of the tsars of Russia. Their shotgun is, to my knowledge, the only item to have survived into the present.

PRINCIPAL BOY (p. 52) — My friend the poet and critic P. J. Kavanagh, was kind enough to comment, 'Are there still those wonderful long-legged thigh-slappers wooing, so nobly, the utterly feminine Maid Marian?'

IN THE BREAK (p.65) — Really a Lawrentian 'pansy'. Billboards and advertising signs in the streets seem to me to be the graffiti of the rich and powerful. The work of the paint-sprayer (done with increasing indulgence and diminishing point: graffiti used to be so much rarer and more cogent than it is now) constitutes an unintelligent tit-for-tat by the poor: you give us your s—, we'll give you ours. The Berlin Wall slogan adopted the methods of the paint-sprayer, and exemplified the relationship.